Lerner SPORTS

GREATEST OF ALL TIME TEAMS

G.O.A.T.
WOMEN'S BASKETBALL TEAMS

MATT DOEDEN

Lerner Publications ◆ Minneapolis

Copyright © 2021 by Lerner Publishing Group, Inc.

All rights reserved. International copyright secured. No part of this book may be reproduced, stored in a retrieval system, or transmitted in any form or by any means—electronic, mechanical, photocopying, recording, or otherwise—without the prior written permission of Lerner Publishing Group, Inc., except for the inclusion of brief quotations in an acknowledged review.

Lerner Publications Company
An imprint of Lerner Publishing Group, Inc.
241 First Avenue North
Minneapolis, MN 55401 USA

For reading levels and more information, look up this title at www.lernerbooks.com.

Main body text set in Aptifer Sans LT Pro. Typeface provided by Linotype AG.

Editor: Shee Yang Designer: Kimberly Morales Photo Editor: Rebecca Higgins Lerner team: Sue Marquis

Library of Congress Cataloging-in-Publication Data

Names: Doeden, Matt, author.
Title: G.O.A.T. Women's Basketball Teams / Matt Doeden.
Other titles: Women's basketball greatest of all time
Description: Minneapolis : Lerner Publications, 2021. | Series: Greatest of all time teams | Includes bibliographical references and index. | Audience: Ages 7–9 | Audience: Grades 2–3 | Summary: "From the Minnesota Lynx to the Phoenix Mercury, which women's basketball team is the greatest? Follow along in this fun and informational ranking to see which team is number one"— Provided by publisher.
Identifiers: LCCN 2020012432 (print) | LCCN 2020012433 (ebook) | ISBN 9781728404455 (library binding) | ISBN 9781728418278 (ebook)
Subjects: LCSH: Basketball—United States—History—Juvenile literature. | Basketball teams—United States—History—Juvenile literature. | Women basketball players—United States—History—Juvenile literature.
Classification: LCC GV885.1 .D654 2021 (print) | LCC GV885.1 (ebook) | DDC 796.323082—dc23

LC record available at https://lccn.loc.gov/2020012432
LC ebook record available at https://lccn.loc.gov/2020012433

Manufactured in the United States of America
1-48503-49017-9/2/2020

TABLE OF CONTENTS

STANDING OUT

Nothing beats the thrill of a basketball game. It's the clutch shots, the tight defense, and the up-and-down pace of play that keeps fans on the edges of their seats. Such stars as Candace Parker, Cynthia Cooper, and Maya Moore have led some of the greatest women's teams in sports history.

FACTS AT A GLANCE

>> In 2019, the Washington Mystics won their first Women's National Basketball Association (WNBA) title after 21 seasons. They outscored the Connecticut Sun 27–14 in the fourth quarter of the final game for a victory.

>> The 2010 Seattle Storm didn't lose a single game in the playoffs. They went 7–0 to win the franchise's second WNBA title.

>> The Olympic Games included women's basketball for the first time in 1976. The Soviet Union dominated, winning all of its games to claim the gold medal.

>> In 2001, the Los Angeles Sparks won 18 games in a row, a WNBA record.

>> The Houston Comets won the first four WNBA championships. In 1998, they went 27–3, the best winning percentage in league history.

In the early days of basketball, men dominated headlines. But that began to change in the 1990s. The popularity of women's basketball boomed. The WNBA started play in 1997, giving fans a new way to cheer on their favorite teams and players.

As the years passed, the league grew. Fans watched dynasties rise and fall. They saw superstars step up their games and become legends. Meanwhile, the international game also rose in popularity. National teams battled for gold and glory at the Olympic Games and other tournaments.

Members of Team USA celebrate after receiving Olympic gold medals in 1996.

Seattle Storm player Breanna Stewart takes a long shot during a 2018 WNBA game against the Minnesota Lynx.

But how do we rank the best of the best? What makes teams that are the greatest of all time (G.O.A.T.) stand out? Is it superstar players and record-setting performances? Or do playoff success and championships matter more?

You must weigh many factors when choosing your G.O.A.T. How do you compare teams from different eras? How do you compare the accomplishments of a WNBA team against those of a national team? What defines greatness to you?

Connecticut Sun center Margo Dydek outreaches an opponent for the ball.

NO. 10

2005 CONNECTICUT SUN

The 2005 Connecticut Sun were the greatest team in women's basketball to not win a championship. The Sun were a dominant force during the regular season. Lindsay Whalen, Nykesha Sales, and Taj McWilliams-Franklin led a

Nykesha Sales avoids defenders to score a basket for Connecticut.

The Sun started the season 12–2 and just kept winning. They finished with the best record in the WNBA at 26–8. They swept both the Detroit Shock and the Indiana Fever in the playoffs to advance to the WNBA Finals.

But that's as far as they could go. The Sacramento Monarchs shocked the Sun in the Finals, three games to one. Connecticut dominated almost every team in the WNBA, but they failed in their quest to win it all.

2005 SUN STATS

>>> The Sun won their regular-season games by an average of 6.8 points.

>>> They won the Eastern Conference by five games over the Fever.

>>> They went 14–3 in home games.

>>> Nykesha Sales led the team with 15.6 points per game (PPG).

>>> Lindsay Whalen averaged a team-high 5.1 assists per game (APG).

Elena Delle Donne puts up a shot. She won the WNBA Most Valuable Player (MVP) award in 2015 and 2019.

NO. 9 2019 WASHINGTON MYSTICS

The 2019 season was magical for the Washington Mystics. After 21 years, the franchise had never won a WNBA title. But the high-scoring trio of Elena Delle Donne, Emma Meesseman, and Kristi Toliver changed that.

The Mystics didn't start the season great. They were just 9–6 after 15 games. But then they caught fire, finishing the season with a scorching 17–2 run. They beat the Las Vegas Aces to advance to the WNBA Finals. It was a thrilling, back-and-forth matchup with the Sun. The Mystics trailed entering the fourth quarter of the winner-take-all fifth game. But they roared back, outscoring Connecticut 27–14 in the fourth quarter to claim their first WNBA title.

Emma Meesseman

2019 MYSTICS STATS

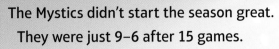

▸▸▸ The Mystics went 14–3 in home games.

▸▸▸ They outscored their opponents by an average of 12 points during the regular season.

▸▸▸ Elena Delle Donne led the team with 19.5 PPG and 8.2 rebounds per game (RPG).

▸▸▸ Kristi Toliver's 5.9 APG led the team.

▸▸▸ Emma Meesseman averaged 17.8 points, 4.6 rebounds, and 1.8 assists in the Finals and was named Finals MVP.

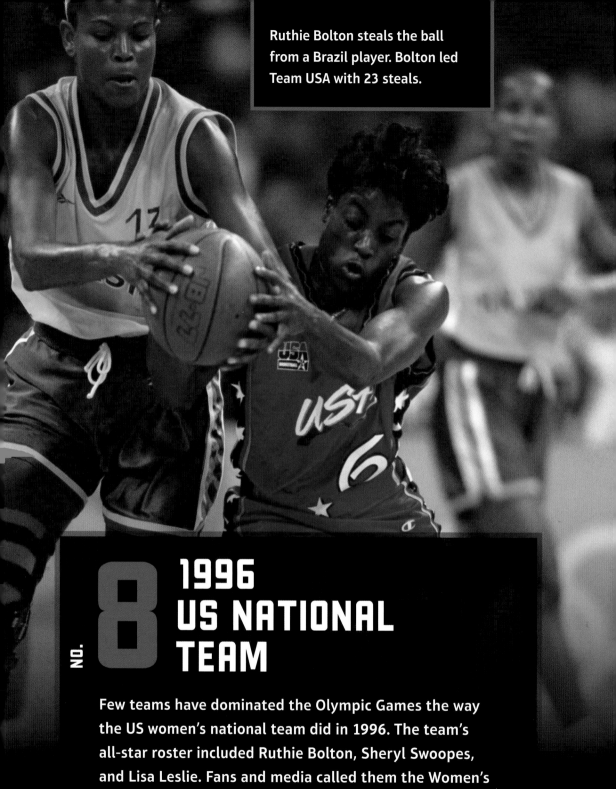

Ruthie Bolton steals the ball from a Brazil player. Bolton led Team USA with 23 steals.

NO. 8

1996 US NATIONAL TEAM

Few teams have dominated the Olympic Games the way the US women's national team did in 1996. The team's all-star roster included Ruthie Bolton, Sheryl Swoopes, and Lisa Leslie. Fans and media called them the Women's Basketball Dream Team.

In the group round, the US women crushed every team in their path. They rolled into the knockout round undefeated, and everyone expected them to keep rolling to the gold medal.

That's just what the US did. They beat Japan and Australia. Then the Dream Team topped Brazil to win the gold medal. Perhaps no team in women's basketball history has had a bigger impact on the sport. Their performance boosted interest in women's basketball, and the WNBA formed the next year.

Sheryl Swoopes

1996 US NATIONAL TEAM STATS

>>> The Women's Basketball Dream Team went 8–0 in the Olympics.

>>> They outscored their opponents 507–339 in the group round.

>>> They set an Olympic record by averaging 102.4 PPG.

>>> From the time the US national team started playing together in 1995 through the Olympic Games, they went 60–0.

>>> A total of 32,987 fans packed the Georgia Dome in Atlanta to watch the gold medal game.

Sylvia Fowles grabs a rebound for the Minnesota Lynx during Game 5 of the 2017 WNBA Finals.

2017 MINNESOTA LYNX

With Seimone Augustus, Lindsay Whalen, Maya Moore, and Sylvia Fowles, the Minnesota Lynx built one of the greatest dynasties in the WNBA during the 2010s. They won four championships during the decade. The 2017 team was the best of them.

Lynx players celebrate with the 2017 WNBA championship trophy.

The Lynx opened the season with nine straight wins. They cruised to a league-best record of 27–7, beating the Los Angeles Sparks by a single game in the Western Conference. They swept the Washington Mystics in the playoffs to advance to the WNBA Finals.

Minnesota faced the Sparks in the Finals. It was a rematch of the 2016 Finals, which the Sparks won. This time, the Lynx came out on top. Fowles led the way. She averaged 18.6 PPG and 13.1 RPG in the playoffs and was named Finals MVP.

2017 LYNX STATS

>>> During the regular season, they beat the Indiana Fever 111–52. The 59-point victory was the biggest blowout in WNBA history.

>>> The Lynx went 15–2 in home games.

>>> Minnesota won by an average of 11.2 points in the regular season.

>>> They went 20–2 in their first 22 games that season.

>>> It was Minnesota's fourth championship in seven seasons.

Svetlana Abrosimova controls the ball for the Seattle Storm.

6 2010 SEATTLE STORM

The Seattle Storm were one of the WNBA's best teams. They made the playoffs for five straight seasons. But they were knocked out in the first round all five times.

The team had three of the league's biggest stars, Sue Bird, Lauren Jackson, and Swin Cash. In 2010, the trio used lights-out shooting to lift the Storm to a league-best 28–6 record. But they knew that the postseason would tell their story.

This time, there was no first-round exit. The Storm tore through the playoffs in what may be the greatest postseason show in WNBA history. The Storm were nearly perfect. They swept the Los Angeles Sparks, Phoenix Mercury, and Atlanta Dream to win the WNBA title. Their postseason performance secured their place as one of the greatest teams in WNBA history.

Swin Cash

2010 STORM STATS

>>> They won 22 of their first 24 games.

>>> Seattle won 13 games in a row from June 18 to July 30.

>>> They went 17–0 at home, becoming the first WNBA team to win all of their home games.

>>> The Storm won the Western Conference by 13 games over the Mercury.

>>> Lauren Jackson led the team with 20.5 PPG and was named the league's MVP.

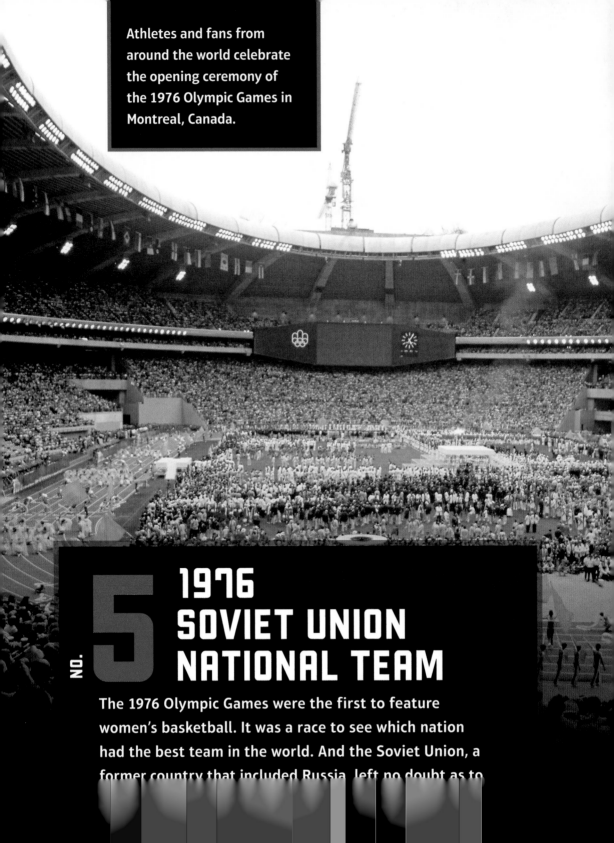

Athletes and fans from around the world celebrate the opening ceremony of the 1976 Olympic Games in Montreal, Canada.

NO. 5

1976 SOVIET UNION NATIONAL TEAM

The 1976 Olympic Games were the first to feature women's basketball. It was a race to see which nation had the best team in the world. And the Soviet Union, a former country that included Russia, left no doubt as to

The Soviet Union's Uljana Semjonova was the tallest player on the team.

Only six teams competed in the tournament. Each team played every other team once. The Soviets destroyed Canada 115–51 in the first game. It was the beginning of pure domination. No one could slow down the Soviet offense. The Soviet Union beat Team USA 112–77 in the second-to-last game. Then the Soviets beat Japan to win the gold medal.

The Soviet Union won gold again in 1980, delivering yet another devastating performance. But the 1976 team started it all and ranks high on any list of the G.O.A.T.

1976 SOVIET UNION NATIONAL TEAM STATS

▶▶▶ The Soviet team hadn't lost a game in a major international competition since 1958.

▶▶▶ The Soviet Union outscored their opponents 504–346 in the tournament.

▶▶▶ Center Uljana Semjonova stood about 7 feet 2 (2.2 m) tall. She led the team with 19.4 PPG and 12.4 RPG.

▶▶▶ Tatyana Ovechkina averaged 12.8 PPG in the tournament.

▶▶▶ The Soviet Union won the first two Olympic gold medals in women's basketball, in 1976 and 1980.

Mwadi Mabika tries to score for Los Angeles against a group of defenders.

NO. 4

2001 LOS ANGELES SPARKS

The best team of the early 2000s was the Los Angeles Sparks, and 2001 was their finest season. Center Lisa Leslie was the heart of the team. Leslie was a force inside, powering her way to baskets and rebounds. Mwadi Mabika and DeLisha Milton-Jones provided the scoring punch from outside. And Tamecka Dixon and Ukari Figgs both dished out 3.9 or more APG.

The Sparks were at their best on their home court. They were a perfect 16–0 in home games during the regular season. They cruised to a 28–4 record, the best in the league. Their dominance carried through to the playoffs. The Sparks went 6–1 and defeated the Charlotte Sting to claim their first WNBA title. Then, in 2002, they won it again. Their brief dynasty helped boost the popularity of the young WNBA and paved the way for future generations of women's basketball.

Lisa Leslie

2001 SPARKS STATS

>>> The Sparks won their first nine games of the regular season.

>>> They had an 18-game winning streak from June 26 to August 11.

>>> The Sparks won the Western Conference by eight games over the Sacramento Monarchs.

>>> Lisa Leslie led the team with 19.5 PPG and 9.6 RPG. She was named the league's MVP.

>>> They ended the Houston Comets' four-year reign as WNBA champions.

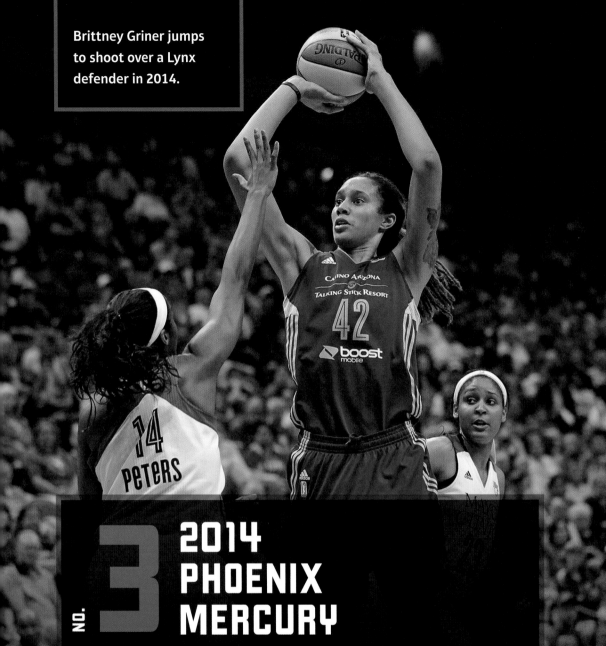

Brittney Griner jumps to shoot over a Lynx defender in 2014.

3

2014 PHOENIX MERCURY

The 2014 Phoenix Mercury had it all. Diana Taurasi was one of the greatest players in WNBA history. Penny Taylor could do a little bit of everything. And second-year center Brittney Griner's size and physical play gave the Mercury the extra edge they needed.

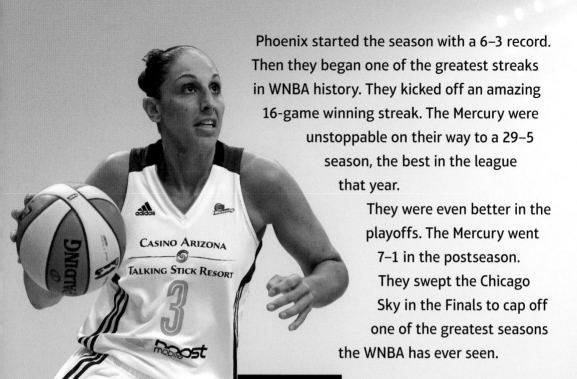

Phoenix started the season with a 6–3 record. Then they began one of the greatest streaks in WNBA history. They kicked off an amazing 16-game winning streak. The Mercury were unstoppable on their way to a 29–5 season, the best in the league that year.

They were even better in the playoffs. The Mercury went 7–1 in the postseason. They swept the Chicago Sky in the Finals to cap off one of the greatest seasons the WNBA has ever seen.

Diana Taurasi

2014 MERCURY STATS

>>> Diana Taurasi led the team with 16.2 PPG and 5.6 APG.

>>> They won by an average of 9.4 PPG.

>>> Brittney Griner blocked 24 shots in seven playoff games.

>>> They outscored the Chicago Sky in the WNBA Finals 267–212.

>>> The Mercury won the franchise's third WNBA championship.

Members of Team USA stand together during the 2016 Olympic women's basketball medal ceremony.

NO. 2

2016 US NATIONAL TEAM

The roster of the 2016 US national team was loaded with the biggest stars in the game. Diana Taurasi, Maya Moore, Elena Delle Donne, and Brittney Griner were just a few of the names on the star-studded roster.

Team USA went to the Olympic Games in Brazil with big expectations from fans. And the team delivered. The US was nearly perfect in the group round. They outscored their

Maya Moore looks for an open teammate.

The victories kept coming in the knockout round. Nobody even came close to beating the powerful Americans. They steamrolled Japan and France to reach the gold-medal match. Lindsay Whalen led the way with 17 points as Team USA crushed Spain to take home gold. It was basketball at its finest. No international team in history has ever been more dominant.

2016 US NATIONAL TEAM STATS

>>> Diana Taurasi was Team USA's leading scorer in the Olympics. She averaged 15.6 PPG.

>>> Maya Moore dished out a team-high 34 assists.

>>> Team USA averaged 102.1 PPG. Their opponents averaged 64.9 PPG.

>>> They beat Spain 101–72 in the gold medal game.

>>> Team USA won their sixth straight Olympic gold medal.

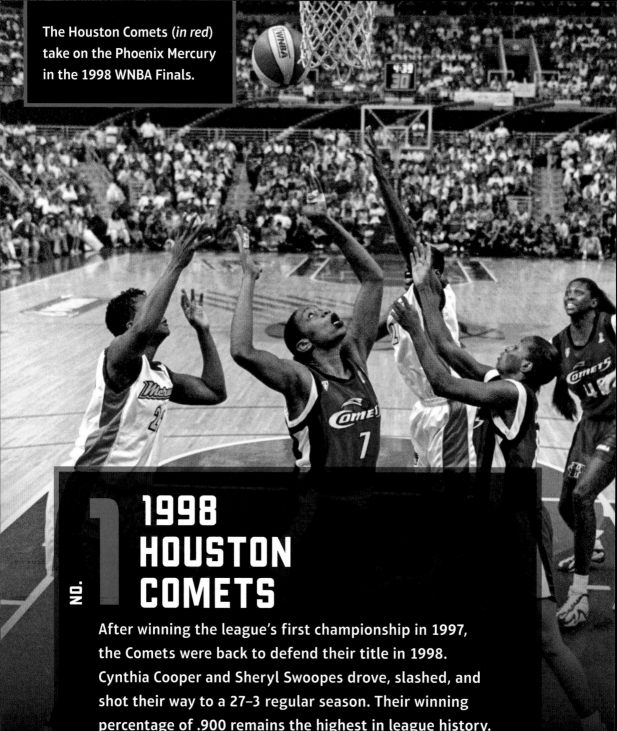

The Houston Comets (*in red*) take on the Phoenix Mercury in the 1998 WNBA Finals.

NO. 1

1998 HOUSTON COMETS

After winning the league's first championship in 1997, the Comets were back to defend their title in 1998. Cynthia Cooper and Sheryl Swoopes drove, slashed, and shot their way to a 27–3 regular season. Their winning percentage of .900 remains the highest in league history.

The Comets swept the Charlotte Sting in the first round of the playoffs to advance to the WNBA Finals. They lost the first game to the Phoenix Mercury. But then Cooper took over. She was unstoppable as Houston won the next two games and claimed their second straight WNBA championship. With only four losses all year, the Comets staked their claim as the greatest women's basketball team of all time.

Cynthia Cooper scored 50 total points in the last two games of the 1998 WNBA Finals.

1998 COMETS STATS

▶▶▶ The Comets had a combined regular season and playoff record of 31–4.

▶▶▶ They won 15 games in a row from June 27 to July 30.

▶▶▶ Cynthia Cooper averaged 22.7 PPG and was named the league's MVP.

▶▶▶ The Comets won the WNBA's Western Conference by eight games over the Phoenix Mercury.

▶▶▶ They went on to win four straight championships from 1997 through 2000.

YOUR G.O.A.T.

NOW THAT YOU'VE READ ABOUT SOME OF THE GREATEST WOMEN'S BASKETBALL TEAMS OF ALL TIME, YOU CAN MAKE YOUR OWN LIST. **Do you agree with our choices? Which teams do you think should be ranked higher? Which don't belong on the list at all? The fun part about G.O.A.T. lists is that there's no right answer. You can decide for yourself which team is the G.O.A.T.**

How will you organize your own list? Do your research. Look at the stats. Which teams set amazing records? Which dominated in the regular season? And how did they do in the biggest games? Sort your list, and choose the greatest basketball teams of all time. Ask a friend or family member to do the same, and then compare. Where do you agree? Where do you disagree, and why? Discuss your rankings and defend your choices. Debating top 10 lists is half the fun!

And don't stop there! What other G.O.A.T. lists can you make? How about the top 10 players or head coaches? Or the 10 greatest games of all time? It's all up to you!

>>> The first game of basketball was played in 1891. The players shot at peach baskets and had to get the ball from the basket after each score.

>>> Diana Taurasi has scored 8,549 points through the 2019 season. That's the most in WNBA history.

>>> Liz Cambage holds the record for most points in a pro game. She scored 53 points for the Dallas Wings in a 2018 game.

>>> The United States has won eight Olympic gold medals in women's basketball, the most in Olympic history.

>>> The Detroit Shock pulled off the biggest comeback in WNBA history in 2005. They trailed the Los Angeles Sparks by 25 points but stormed back to a shocking 79–73 win.

GLOSSARY

center: the player who usually plays near the basket

clutch: successful in an important situation

comeback: a game or series in which a team that is trailing charges back to win

dominate: to completely control an opponent

dynasty: a long period of dominance by a team, usually including multiple championships

franchise: the entire organization of a team

group round: the part of a tournament where teams are split into groups and each team plays every other team

knockout round: the part of a tournament where the winner advances and the loser is knocked out of the tournament

rebound: to gain possession of the ball after a missed shot

LEARN MORE

Basketball Reference
https://www.basketball-reference.com/

Levit, Joseph. *Basketball's G.O.A.T.: Michael Jordan, LeBron James, and More*. Minneapolis: Lerner Publications, 2020.

The Official Site of the WNBA
https://www.wnba.com/

Scheff, Matt. *NBA and WNBA Finals*. Minneapolis: Lerner Publications, 2021.

Sports Illustrated Kids: Basketball
https://www.sikids.com/basketball

Wendel, S. E. *The WNBA Finals*. New York: Smartbook Media, 2018.

INDEX

PHOTO ACKNOWLEDGMENTS

Image credits: Jayne Kamin-Oncea/Getty Images, p. 1; AP Photo/Mark J. Terrill, p. 4; AP Photo/Susan Ragan, p. 6; Nick Wosika/Icon Sportswire/AP Photo, p. 7; Jed Jacobsohn/Getty Images, pp. 8, 9; G Fiume/Getty Images, pp. 10, 11; Doug Pensinger/Getty Images, pp. 12, 13; Hannah Foslien/Getty Images, pp. 14, 15; Scott Cunningham/NBAE/Getty Images, pp. 16, 17; Tony Duffy/Allsport/ Getty Images, p. 18; Bettmann/Getty Images, p. 19; Jeff Gross /Allsport/Getty Images, p. 20; Harry How/Allsport/Getty Images, p. 21; AP Photo/Stacy Bengs, p. 22; Bruce Yeung/Icon Sports Wire/Getty Images, p. 23; Tim Clayton - Corbis/ Getty Images, pp. 24, 25; Todd Warshaw/Getty Images, pp. 26, 27; Pongnathee Kluaythong/EyeEm/Getty Images, p. 28 (basketball). Design elements: ijaydesign99/Shutterstock.com; RaiDztor/Shutterstock.com; MIKHAIL GRACHIKOV/ Shutterstock.com; EFKS/Shutterstock.com; Vitalii Kozyrskyi/Shutterstock.com; ESB Professional/Shutterstock.com; MEandMO/Shutterstock.com; Roman Sotola/ Shutterstock.com.

Cover: Jayne Kamin-Oncea/Getty Images. Design elements: EFKS/Shutterstock. com; RaiDztor/Shutterstock.com; MIKHAIL GRACHIKOV/Shutterstock.com; ijaydesign99/Shutterstock.com.